Preface
머리말

< Day-by-Day Writing Korean Hangeul > is a book for children just starting to learn how to write Hangeul.

Hangeul is the Korean alphabet and was developed using scientific principles. The sounds of its characters are fixed! Unlike Korean, the English alphabet uses different sounds depending on the word spoken, while Chinese characters are mostly based on differences in meaning. Thus the ease of learning Hangeul! If you can't understand what a word in Korean means but have learned Hangeul's fixed sounds, you should still be able to read! Based on this point, I have constructed the following book. I am confident that learners will be quickly assembling words after learning the Hangeul's core sounds and the principles of combining consonants and vowels. In addition, this book teaches the actual construction of Hangeul's characters, step by step, line by line.

A readable language is a meaningful language. It is my hope that the <**Day-by-Day Writing Korean Hangeul**> series will help children learn Korean swiftly and happily.

Author **The Calling**

with special thanks to Christine Ahn

한글 쓰기 학습을 시작한 어린이를 위한 교재
< 하루하루 한글쓰기 >

한글은 한국의 문자이고 과학적인 원리로 개발되었으며, 문자의 소리들은 고정되어 있습니다! 한국어와는 달리, 영어의 알파벳은 단어에 따라 소리가 달라지고, 중국어의 한자는 대부분 의미의 차이에 기반하고 있습니다. 그래서 한글은 배우기 쉽습니다! 한국어 단어의 의미를 모른다 하더라도 한글의 고정된 소리를 배웠으면 읽을 수 있습니다. 이 점에 기인하여, 이 책을 기획하였습니다. 학습자들이 한글의 핵심 소리와 자모음 결합 원리를 배우고 나면 단어를 빠르게 만들 것이라고 자신합니다. 또한 이 책은 한글의 실제적인 구조를 차근차근 가르쳐 주고 있습니다.

읽기 쉬운 언어가 의미 있는 언어입니다. 〈하루하루 한글쓰기〉 시리즈를 통해 아이들이 한국어를 빠르고 즐겁게 익히기를 바랍니다.

저자 더 콜링

About this book
이 책의 특징

The <Day-by-Day Writing Korean Hangeul> series is designed to help learners understand the order in which to write letters and the principles involved.

〈하루하루 한글쓰기〉 시리즈는 글자의 쓰는 순서와 글자가 만들어지는 원리를 이해하고 익숙해지는 것에 중점을 둔 한글 쓰기 전문 교재입니다.

● Learning one-syllable blocks without a final consonant ●
받침 없는 한 글자 따라 쓰기

Consonants + Compound Vowels

Practicing to write one-syllable blocks without a final consonant, in order, using 14 basic consonants, 5 compound consonants and 11 compound vowels.

자음 + 복잡 모음

기본 자음 14개, 쌍자음 5개와 복잡 모음 11개로 이루어진 받침 없는 한 글자를 순서에 맞게 따라 쓰며 익힙니다.

'Review' and 'Exercise' serve to check a learner's understanding.
They are arranged using basic words and illustrations for ease of study.

글자 학습을 위한 익히기와 확인하기는 아이들의 눈높이에 맞춘 기초 낱말을 중심으로
의미 파악에 도움이 되는 그림과 함께 구성하였습니다.

● Various activities ●
다양한 활동

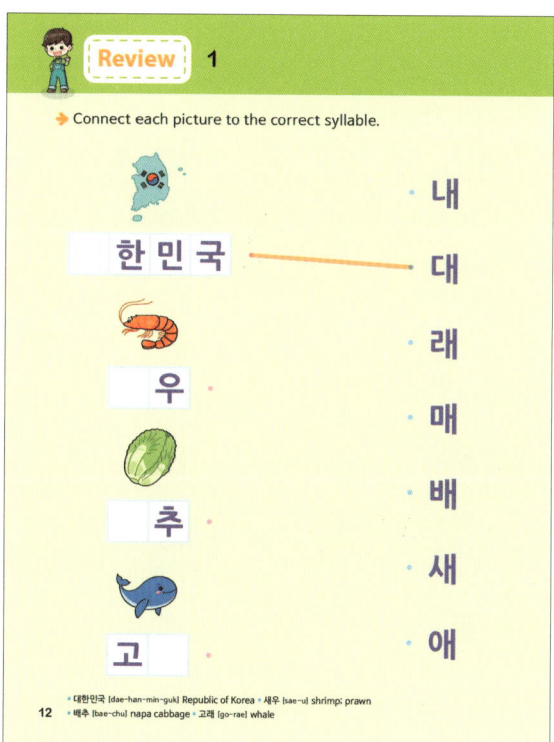

● Completed learning ●
마무리 학습

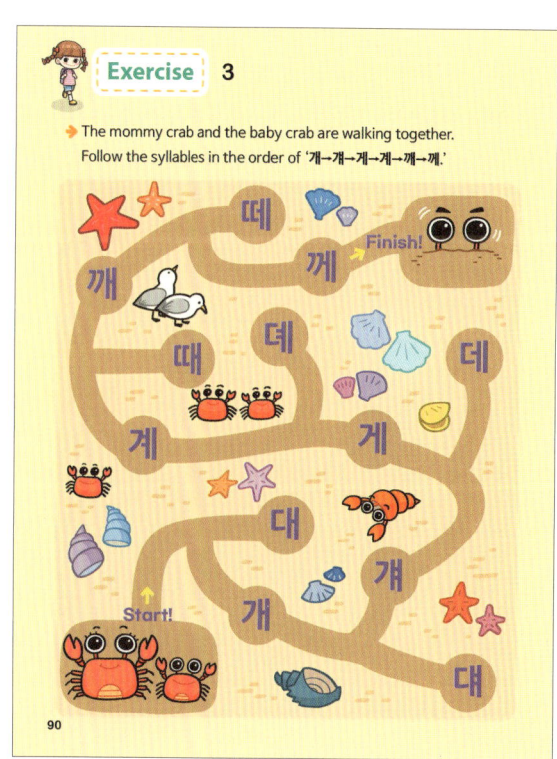

Review

Learning syllables happens in the context of finding directions and hidden characters, crossword puzzles, and other funny activities.

익히기

따라 쓰기 사이에 길 찾기, 숨은 글자 찾기, 십자말풀이 등 다양한 활동을 배치하여 배운 내용을 재미있게 익힙니다.

Exercise

Check your progress with 'Exercise.'

확인하기

마무리 학습으로 앞에서 배운 내용을 총 복습합니다.

Downloading MP3

Practice while listening to the voice of a professional Korean voice actor.

MP3 다운로드 우리말 전문 성우의 정확한 음성을 들으며 학습하세요.

 blog.naver.com
 drive.google.com

Contents
차례

Basic Consonants + Compound Vowels 기본 자음 + 복잡 모음

Basic Consonants + ㅐ	8
Review 1~2	12
Basic Consonants + ㅒ	14
Review 3~4	18
Basic Consonants + ㅔ	20
Review 5~6	24
Basic Consonants + ㅖ	26
Review 7~8	30
Basic Consonants + ㅘ	32
Review 9~10	36
Basic Consonants + ㅙ	38
Review 11~12	42
Basic Consonants + ㅚ	44
Review 13~14	48
Basic Consonants + ㅝ	50
Review 15~16	54
Basic Consonants + ㅞ	56
Review 17~18	60

Basic **Consonants** + ㅟ	62
Review 19~20	66
Basic **Consonants** + ㅢ	68
Review 21~22	72

Compound Consonants + Compound Vowels 쌍자음 + 복잡 모음

Compound **Consonants** + ㅐ	76
Compound **Consonants** + ㅔ	77
Compound **Consonants** + ㅘ	78
Compound **Consonants** + ㅙ	79
Compound **Consonants** + ㅚ	80
Compound **Consonants** + ㅝ	81
Compound **Consonants** + ㅞ	82
Compound **Consonants** + ㅟ	83
Compound **Consonants** + ㅢ	84
Review 23~25	85

Exercise 1~8   88

Writing the syllables   96

Day-by-Day
Writing Korean
Hangeul

Basic Consonants
+ Compound Vowels

기본 자음 + 복잡 모음

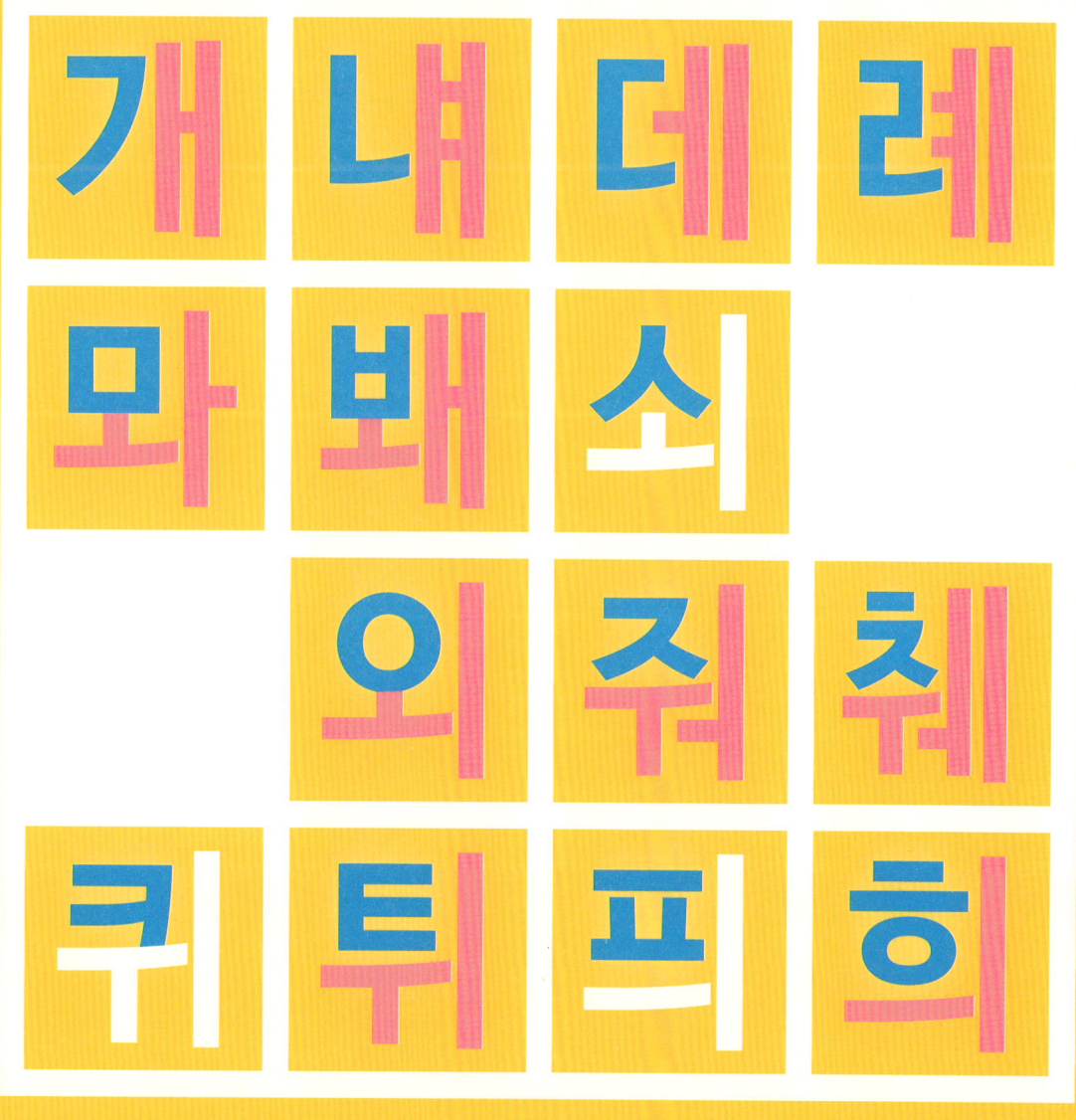

 Read the syllables combining the consonants and the vowel 'ㅐ' and write them in order.

ㄱㅐ [gae]	개	개	개	개
ㄴㅐ [nae]	내	내	내	내
ㄷㅐ [dae]	대	대	대	대

래 [rae]		
매 [mae]		
배 [bae]		

→ Connect each picture to the correct syllable.

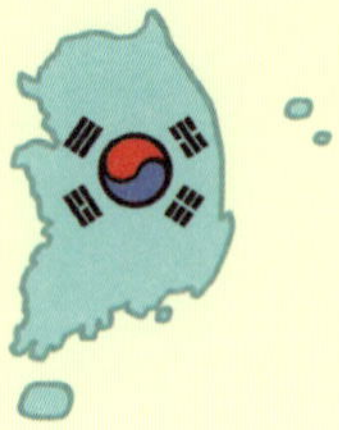

□ 한 민 국 —— 대

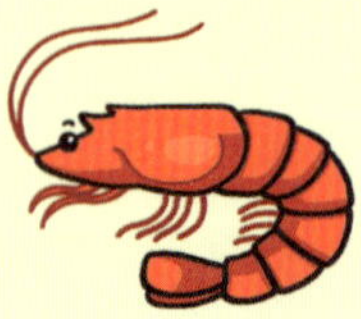

□ 우

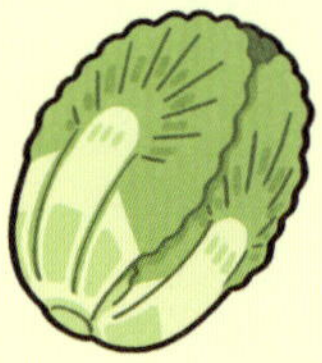

□ 추

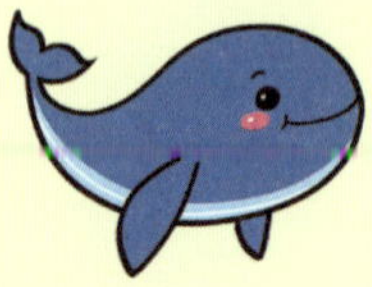

고 □

• 내
• 대
• 래
• 매
• 배
• 새
• 애

* 대한민국 [dae-han-min-guk] Republic of Korea * 새우 [sae-u] shrimp; prawn
* 배추 [bae-chu] napa cabbage * 고래 [go-rae] whale

→ Look at the pictures and write the correct syllables in the boxes.

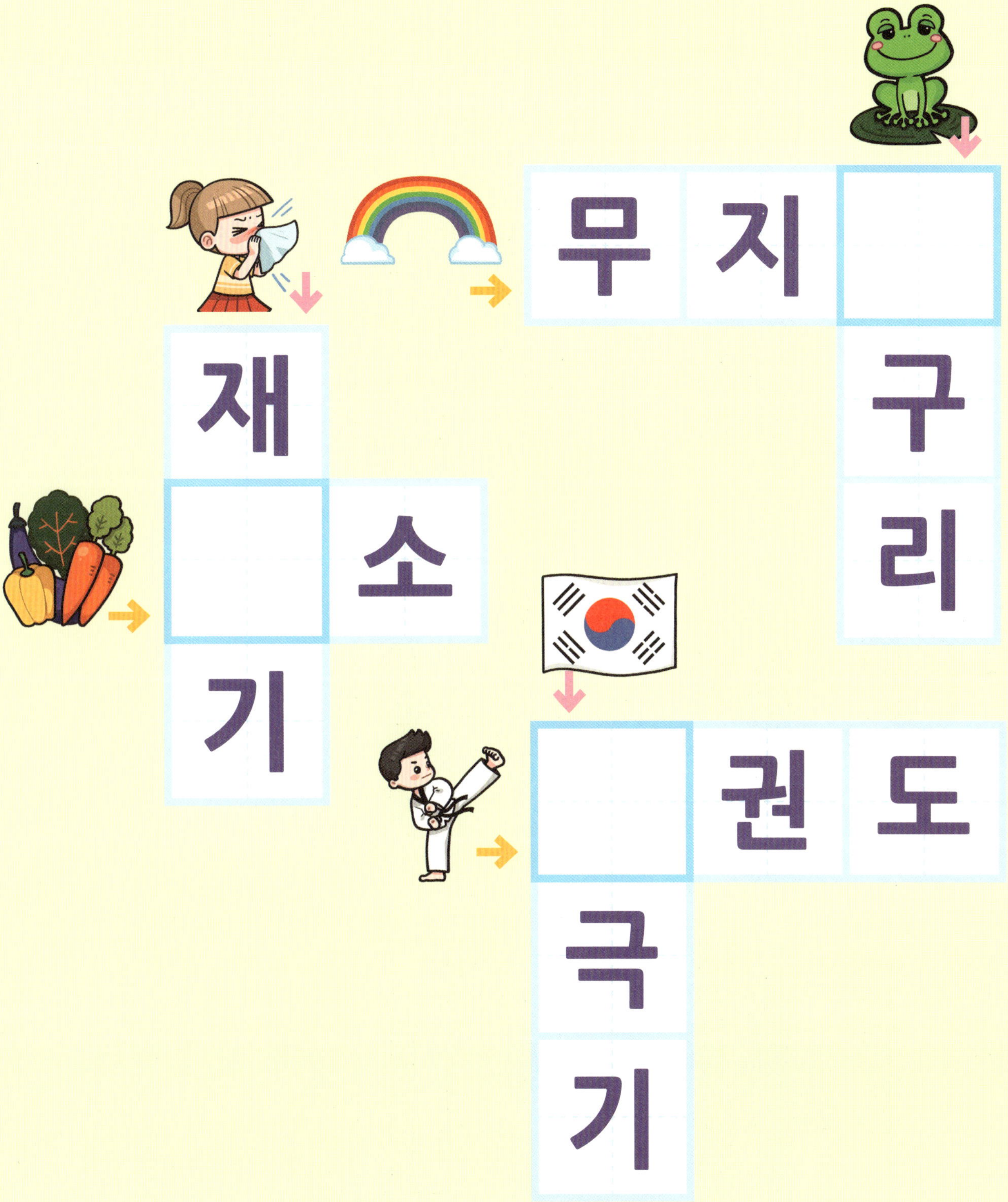

* 무지개 [mu-ji-gae] rainbow * 개구리 [gae-gu-ri] frog * 재채기 [jae-chae-gi] sneeze * 채소 [chae-so] vegetable
* 태권도 [tae-ggwon-do] Taekwondo (Korean traditional sport)
* 태극기 [tae-geuk-ggi] Taegeukgi (the national flag of the Republic of Korea)

개

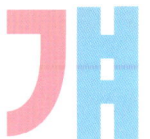

Read the syllables combining the consonants and the vowel 'ㅐ' and write them in order.

ㄱ ㅐ
[gyae]

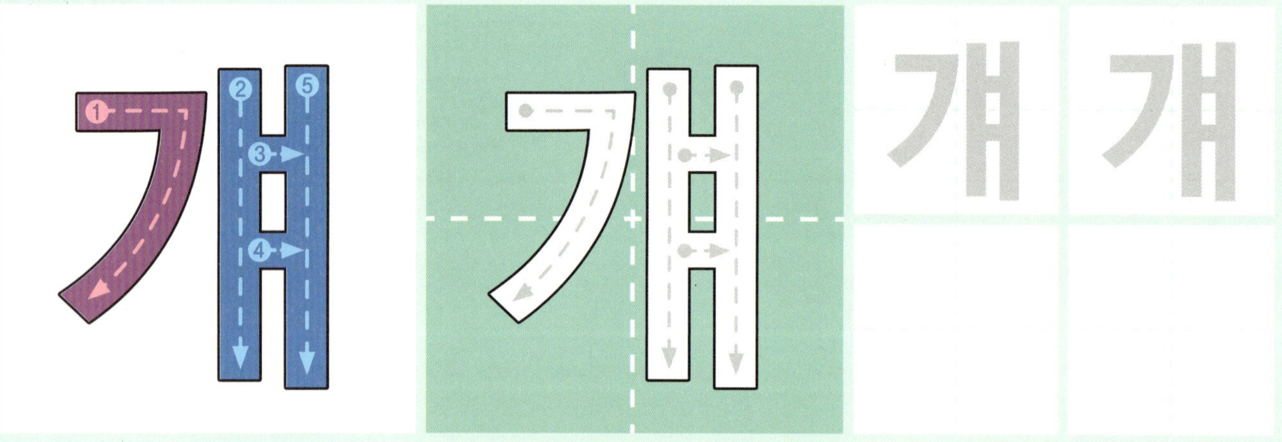

ㄴ ㅐ
[nyae]

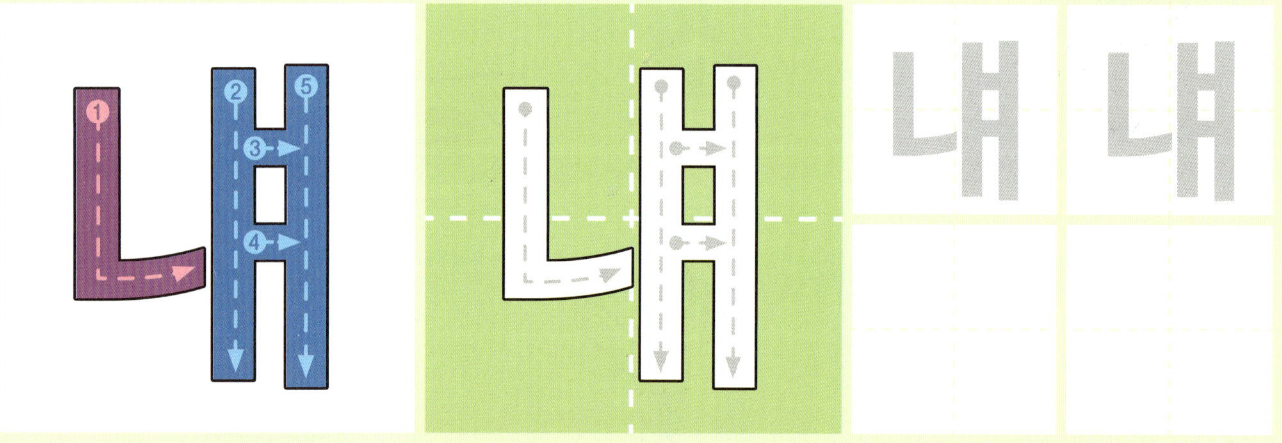

ㄷ ㅐ
[dyae]

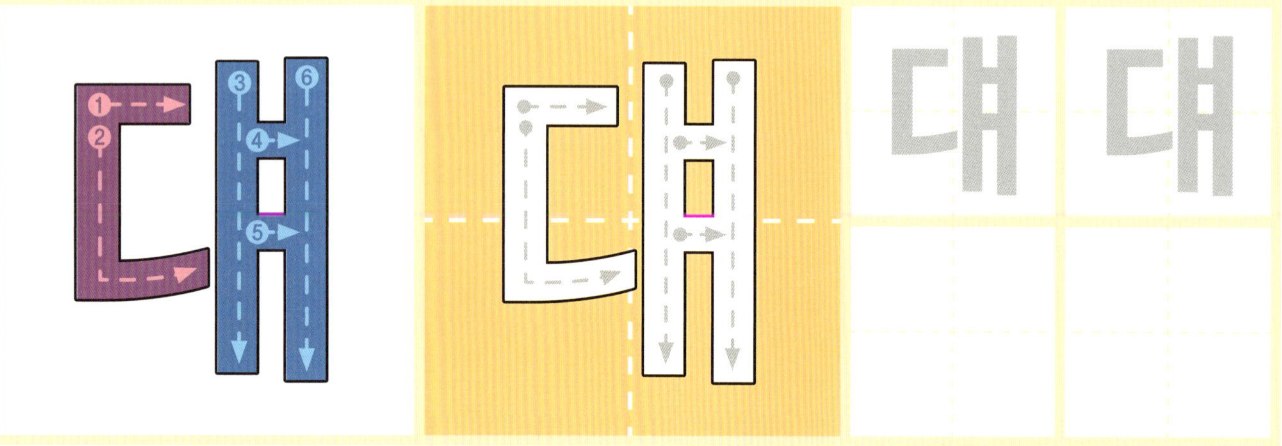

| 래 [ryae] |
| 매 [myae] |
| 배 [byae] |

15

Review 3

→ Which of the 4 syllables will be suitable for the boxes?

개 섀 얘 재

ㅈ + ㅐ =

ㅅ + ㅒ =

ㄱ + ㅐ =

ㅇ + ㅒ =

Review 4

➔ Follow the syllables with the vowel 'ㅐ' to the finish.

Start!

걔	배	매	배
새	대	재	섀
태	래	매	얘
해	래	태	내

Finish!

19

게

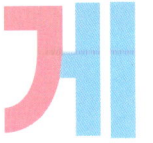

Read the syllables combining the consonants and the vowel 'ㅔ' and write them in order.

ㄱㅔ [ge]	게	게	게	게
ㄴㅔ [ne]	네	네	네	네
ㄷㅔ [de]	데	데	데	데

레 [re]

메 [me]

베 [be]

Review 5

→ Connect each picture to the correct syllable.

　달　・　　　　　・ 레

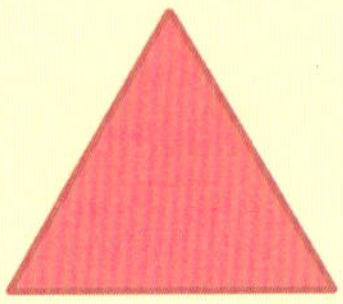

　모　・　　　　　・ 메

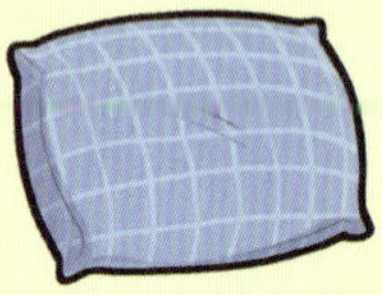

　　　　　　　　　・ 베

　몬　・　　　　　・ 세

　　　　　　　　　・ 에

　개　・　　　　　・ 제

* 메달 [me-dal] medal * 세모 [se-mo] triangle * 레몬 [re-mon] lemon * 베개 [be-gae] pillow

Review 6

→ Look at the pictures and write the correct syllables in the boxes.

* 그네 [geu-ne] swing * 네모 [ne-mo] quadrangle * 세배 [se-bae] New Year's bow
* 세수 [se-su] washing one's face * 스케이트 [seu-ke-i-teu] skate * 케이크 [ke-i-keu] cake

 Read the syllables combining the consonants and the vowel 'ㅖ' and write them in order.

ㄱㅖ [gye]	계	계	계	계
ㄴㅖ [nye]	녜	녜	녜	녜
ㄷㅖ [dye]	뎨	뎨	뎨	뎨

ㄹ ㅖ [rye]	례	례	례	례
ㅁ ㅖ [mye]	몌	몌	몌	몌
ㅂ ㅖ [bye]	볘	볘	볘	볘

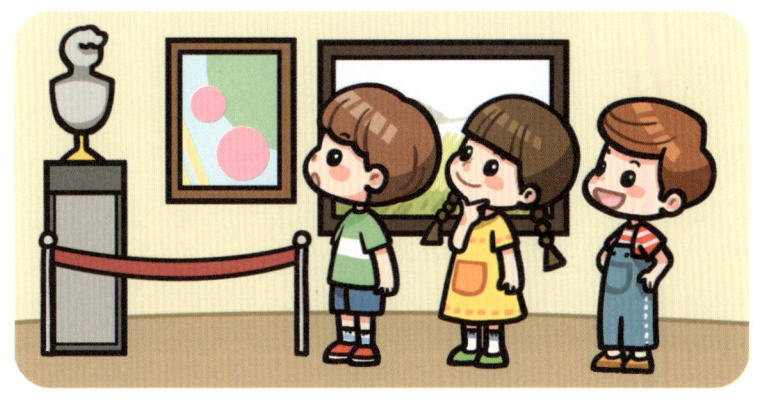

 **Review** 7

→ Which of the 4 syllables will be suitable for the boxes?

레 셰 켸 혜

ㅅ + ㅖ =

ㄹ + ㅖ =

ㅎ + ㅖ =

ㅋ + ㅖ =

Review 8

→ The mailman is delivering the letters.
Find the letters with the vowel 'ㅔ' and circle them.

베 예 세 페

과

Read the syllables combining the consonants and the vowel '**ㅘ**' and write them in order.

ㄱ ㅗ ㅏ [gwa]	과	과	과	과
ㄴ ㅗ ㅏ [nwa]	놔	놔	놔	놔
ㄷ ㅗ ㅏ [dwa]	돠	돠	돠	돠

ㄹ ㅗ ㅏ
[rwa]

롸 롸 롸 롸

ㅁ ㅗ ㅏ
[mwa]

뫄 뫄 뫄 뫄

ㅂ ㅗ ㅏ
[bwa]

봐 봐 봐 봐

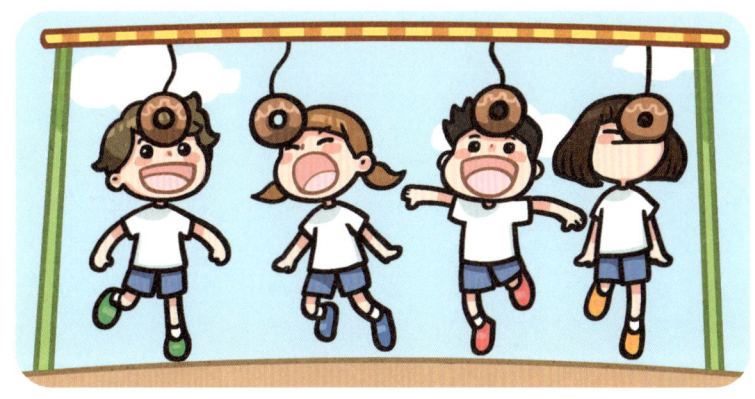

Review 9

→ Which of the 4 syllables will be suitable for the boxes?

놔 와 좌 콰

ㅋ + ㅘ = ☐

ㅇ + ㅘ = ☐

ㄴ + ㅘ = ☐

ㅈ + ㅘ = ☐

Review 10

➡ Connect each picture to the correct syllable.

▢ 석	과
기 ▢ 집	봐
	와
▢ 자	좌
	콰
백 ▢ 점	화

* 좌석 [jwa-seok] seat　* 기와집 [gi-wa-jip] tile-roofed house
* 과자 [gwa-ja] snack　* 백화점 [bae-kwa-jeom] department store

괘

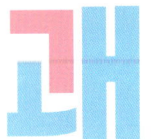

Read the syllables combining the consonants and the vowel **'괘'** and write them in order.

ㄱ ㅗ ㅐ [gwae]	괘	괘	괘	괘
ㄴ ㅗ ㅐ [nwae]	놰	놰	놰	놰
ㄷ ㅗ ㅐ [dwae]	돼	돼	돼	돼

ㄹ ㅐ ㅗ [rwae]	쇄	쇄	쇄 쇄
ㅁ ㅐ ㅗ [mwae]	뫠	뫠	뫠 뫠
ㅂ ㅐ ㅗ [bwae]	봬	봬	봬 봬

Review 11

→ Which of the 4 syllables will be suitable for the boxes?

괘 쇄 왜 홰

ㅅ + ㅙ = ☐

ㅎ + ㅙ = ☐

ㄱ + ㅙ = ☐

ㅇ + ㅙ = ☐

Review 12

→ Follow the syllables with the vowel '왜' to the finish.

Start! 괘	좨	봬	뫼
뇌	되	뢔	쇄
퇴	쾨	뢰	왜
홰 Finish!	돼	쾌	놰

 Read the syllables combining the consonants and the vowel 'ㅚ' and write them in order.

ㄱ ㅣ ㅗ [goe]	괴	괴	괴	괴
ㄴ ㅣ ㅗ [noe]	뇌	뇌	뇌	뇌
ㄷ ㅣ ㅗ [doe]	되	되	되	되

| ㄹ ㅗ ㅣ [roe] | 뢰 | 뢰 | 뢰 뢰 |

| ㅁ ㅗ ㅣ [moe] | 뫼 | 뫼 | 뫼 뫼 |

| ㅂ ㅗ ㅣ [boe] | 뵈 | 뵈 | 뵈 뵈 |

Review 13

→ Connect each picture to the correct syllable.

☐ 고	• 괴
	• 쇠
☐ 물	• 외
	• 죄
참 ☐	• 최
열 ☐	• 회

48 * 최고 [choe-go] the best * 괴물 [goe-mul] monster * 참외 [cha-moe] Oriental melon * 열쇠 [yeol-ssoe] key

Review 14

→ Haha is visiting his mother's parents' home.
Write the correct syllables in the boxes.

와 왜 외

☐할아버지   ☐할머니
                ☐숙모

☐삼촌

* 외할아버지 [oe-ha-ra-beo-ji] mother's father * 외할머니 [oe-hal-meo-ni] mother's mother
* 외삼촌 [oe-sam-chon] mother's brother * 외숙모 [oe-sung-mo] the wife of your mother's brother

 Read the syllables combining the consonants and the vowel 'ㅝ' and write them in order.

ㄱ ㅝ [gwo]	궈	궈	궈	궈
ㄴ ㅝ [nwo]	눠	눠	눠	눠
ㄷ ㅝ [dwo]	둬	둬	둬	둬

ㄹ ㅓ
ㅜ
[rwo] 뤄 뤄 뤄 뤄

ㅁ ㅓ
ㅜ
[mwo] 뭐 뭐 뭐 뭐

ㅂ ㅓ
ㅜ
[bwo] 붜 붜 붜 붜

Review 15

→ Which of the 4 syllables will be suitable for the boxes?

궈 뤄 워 쿼

ㅇ + ㅟ =

ㄱ + ㅟ =

ㅋ + ㅟ =

ㄹ + ㅟ =

Review 16

→ The mother bird brought food for her baby birds.
Circle the baby birds with the vowel 'ㅟ.'

 Read the syllables combining the consonants and the vowel 'ㅞ' and write them in order.

ㄱ ㅞ [gwe]	궤	궤	궤	궤
ㄴ ㅞ [nwe]	눼	눼	눼	눼
ㄷ ㅞ [dwe]	뒈	뒈	뒈	뒈

56

ㄹ ㅜ ㅔ [rwe]	뤠	뤠	뤠	뤠
ㅁ ㅜ ㅔ [mwe]	뭬	뭬	뭬	뭬
ㅂ ㅜ ㅔ [bwe]	붸	붸	붸	붸

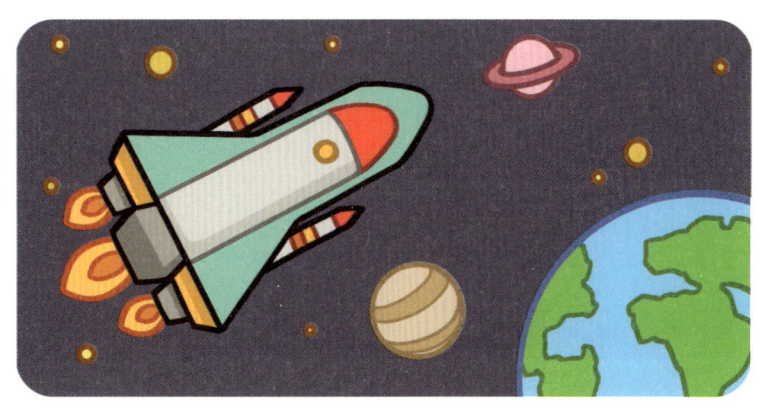

Review 17

→ Which of the 4 syllables will be suitable for the boxes?

궤   뒈   웨   훼

ㅎ + ㅞ =

ㄱ + ㅞ =

ㄷ + ㅞ =

ㅇ + ㅞ =

Review 18

→ Follow the syllables with the vowel '궤' to the finish.

			Start!
워	뉴	쉐	궤
뭬	줴	뒈	쿼
눼	쉬	튀	훠
뤠	붸	퉤	훠
			Finish!

ㅟ

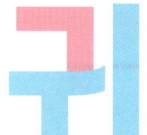

Read the syllables combining the consonants and the vowel 'ㅟ' and write them in order.

ㄱ ㅜ ㅣ [gwi]

귀 귀 귀 귀

ㄴ ㅜ ㅣ [nwi]

뉘 뉘 뉘 뉘

ㄷ ㅜ ㅣ [dwi]

뒤 뒤 뒤 뒤

ㄹ ㅜ ㅣ [rwi]	뤼	뤼	뤼 뤼
ㅁ ㅜ ㅣ [mwi]	뮈	뮈	뮈 뮈
ㅂ ㅜ ㅣ [bwi]	뷔	뷔	뷔 뷔

Review 19

→ Connect each picture to the correct syllable.

샌드 ⬜ 치 •

• 귀
• 쉬
• 위

사 마 ⬜ •

• 쥐
• 취

⬜ 김 •

• 퀴
• 튀

바 ⬜ •

* 샌드위치 [saen-deu-wi-chi] sandwich　* 사마귀 [sa-ma-gwi] mantis
* 튀김 [twi-gim] fried food　* 바퀴 [ba-kwi] wheel

Review 20

→ Ruru and her friends are playing rock-paper-scissors. Circle the winners.

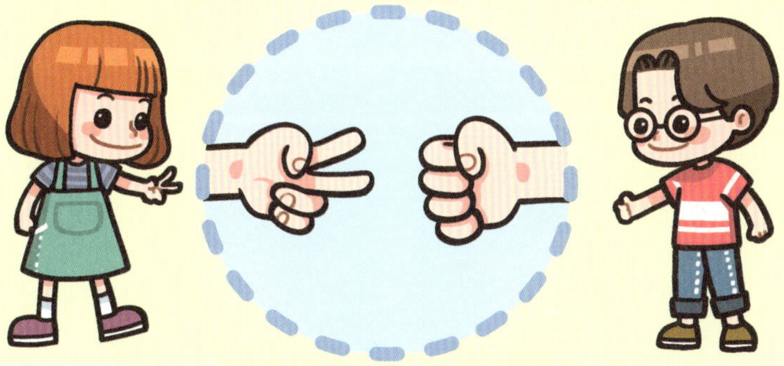

가위　　바위

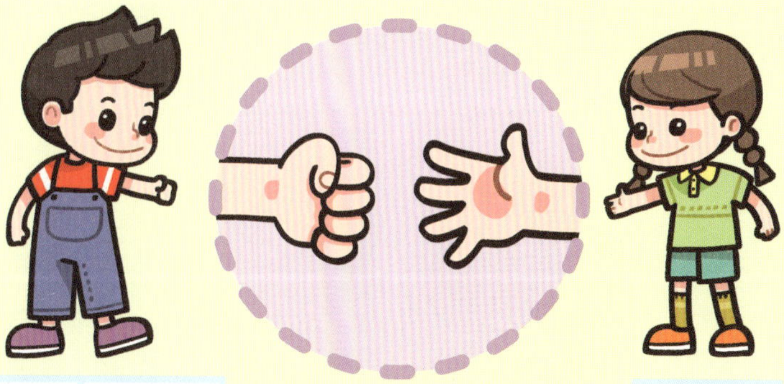

바위　　보

보　　가위

* 가위 [ga-wi] scissors * 바위 [ba-wi] rock * 보 [bo] paper; wrapping cloth

ㅚ

Read the syllables combining the consonants and the vowel 'ㅚ' and write them in order.

[gui]

[nui]

[dui]

68

[rui] 리

[mui] 미

[bui] 비

Review 21

→ Haha and his friends are standing in front of the chairs.
Find the chairs with the syllables '의, 희' and circle them.

Review 22

→ Here are some pretty designs!
Trace the syllables in grey and color the patterns.

Compound Consonants
+ Compound Vowels

쌍자음 + 복잡 모음

 Read the syllables combining the compound consonants and the vowel 'ㅐ' and write them in order.

ㄲㅐ [ggae]	깨	깨	깨	깨	깨
ㄸㅐ [ddae]	때	때	때	때	때
ㅃㅐ [bbae]	빼	빼	빼	빼	빼
ㅆㅐ [ssae]	쌔	쌔	쌔	쌔	쌔
ㅉㅐ [jjae]	째	째	째	째	째

 Read the syllables combining the compound consonants and the vowel 'ㅔ' and write them in order.

ㄲㅔ [gge]	께	께	께	께	께
ㄸㅔ [dde]	떼	떼	떼	떼	떼
ㅃㅔ [bbe]	뻬	뻬	뻬	뻬	뻬
ㅆㅔ [sse]	쎄	쎄	쎄	쎄	쎄
ㅉㅔ [jje]	쩨	쩨	쩨	쩨	쩨

 Read the syllables combining the compound consonants and the vowel '과' and write them in order.

ㄲ ㅏ ㅗ [ggwa]	꽈	꽈	꽈	꽈	꽈
ㄸ ㅏ ㅗ [ddwa]	똬	똬	똬	똬	똬
ㅃ ㅏ ㅗ [bbwa]	뽜	뽜	뽜	뽜	뽜
ㅆ ㅏ ㅗ [sswa]	쏴	쏴	쏴	쏴	쏴
ㅉ ㅏ ㅗ [jjwa]	쫘	쫘	쫘	쫘	쫘

꽤

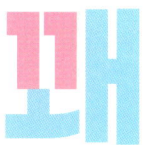

Read the syllables combining the compound consonants and the vowel '괘' and write them in order.

ㄲ ㅗ ㅐ [ggwae]	꽤	꽤	꽤	꽤	꽤
ㄸ ㅗ ㅐ [ddwae]	뙈	뙈	뙈	뙈	뙈
ㅃ ㅗ ㅐ [bbwae]	뽸	뽸	뽸	뽸	뽸
ㅆ ㅗ ㅐ [sswae]	쐐	쐐	쐐	쐐	쐐
ㅉ ㅗ ㅐ [jjwae]	쫴	쫴	쫴	쫴	쫴

 Read the syllables combining the compound consonants and the vowel '괴' and write them in order.

ㄲ ㅗ ㅣ [ggoe]	꾀	꾀	꾀 꾀 꾀	
ㄸ ㅗ ㅣ [ddoe]	뙤	뙤	뙤 뙤 뙤	
ㅃ ㅗ ㅣ [bboe]	뾔	뾔	뾔 뾔 뾔	
ㅆ ㅗ ㅣ [ssoe]	쐬	쐬	쐬 쐬 쐬	
ㅉ ㅗ ㅣ [jjoe]	쬐	쬐	쬐 쬐 쬐	

 Read the syllables combining the compound consonants and the vowel 'ㅟ' and write them in order.

ㄲ ㅜ ㅓ [ggwo]	꿔	꿔	꿔	꿔	꿔
ㄸ ㅜ ㅓ [ddwo]	뚸	뚸	뚸	뚸	뚸
ㅃ ㅜ ㅓ [bbwo]	뿨	뿨	뿨	뿨	뿨
ㅆ ㅜ ㅓ [sswo]	쒀	쒀	쒀	쒀	쒀
ㅉ ㅜ ㅓ [jjwo]	쭤	쭤	쭤	쭤	쭤

 Read the syllables combining the compound consonants and the vowel '궤' and write them in order.

ㄲ+ㅞ [ggwe]	꿰	꿰	꿰	꿰	꿰
ㄸ+ㅞ [ddwe]	뛔	뛔	뛔	뛔	뛔
ㅃ+ㅞ [bbwe]	쀄	쀄	쀄	쀄	쀄
ㅆ+ㅞ [sswe]	쒜	쒜	쒜	쒜	쒜
ㅉ+ㅞ [jjwe]	쮀	쮀	쮀	쮀	쮀

뀌

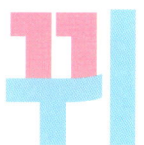

Read the syllables combining the compound consonants and the vowel 'ㅟ' and write them in order.

ㄲ ㅜ ㅣ [ggwi]	뀌	뀌	뀌	뀌	뀌
ㄸ ㅜ ㅣ [ddwi]	뛰	뛰	뛰	뛰	뛰
ㅃ ㅜ ㅣ [bbwi]	쀠	쀠	쀠	쀠	쀠
ㅆ ㅜ ㅣ [sswi]	쒸	쒸	쒸	쒸	쒸
ㅉ ㅜ ㅣ [jjwi]	쮜	쮜	쮜	쮜	쮜

ㄲㅢ

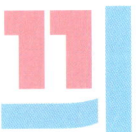

Read the syllables combining the compound consonants and the vowel 'ㅢ' and write them in order.

ㄲ ㅡ ㅣ [ggui]	끠	끠	끠	끠	끠
ㄸ ㅡ ㅣ [ddui]	띄	띄	띄	띄	띄
ㅃ ㅡ ㅣ [bbui]	쁴	쁴	쁴	쁴	쁴
ㅆ ㅡ ㅣ [ssui]	씌	씌	씌	씌	씌
ㅉ ㅡ ㅣ [jjui]	쯰	쯰	쯰	쯰	쯰

Review 23

→ Which of the 4 syllables will be suitable for the boxes?

깨 께 꽈 꾀

ㄲ + ㅚ =

ㄲ + ㅔ =

ㄲ + ㅘ =

ㄲ + ㅐ =

Review 24

→ Ruru has to get out of the twisted maze! Follow the syllables in the order of '꽈→똬→빠→쏴→쫘.' Read the syllables as you go!

Review 25

→ Connect each picture to the correct syllable.

주근 •   • 깨
         • 때
꼬리 •   • 빼
         • 꾀
널   기 • • 쬐
         • 뛰
올   미 • • 쒸

* 주근깨 [ju-geun-ggae] freckle　* 꾀꼬리 [ggoe-ggo-ri] nightingale
* 널뛰기 [neol-ddwi-gi] riding a standing see-saw (a traditional Korean game)　* 올빼미 [ol-bbae-mi] owl

87

Exercise 1

→ What are the missing syllables?
Write the correct syllables in the bulbs.

| 개 | | 대 | 래 |

| 세 | 에 | | 체 |

| 돠 | 롸 | 뫄 | |

| 봬 | | 왜 | 좨 |

88

Exercise 2

→ What are the missing syllables?
Write the correct syllables on the chunks of food.

쿼 　 퓌 휘

위 쥐 　 퀴

께 떼 뻬 　

꾀 　 쀠 쒸

Exercise 3

→ The mommy crab and the baby crab are walking together. Follow the syllables in the order of '개→걔→게→계→깨→께.'

Exercise 4

→ The Bluebird is looking for its home.
Follow the syllables in the order of '새→섀→세→셰→쌔→쎄.'

Exercise 5

→ These are one-syllable words.
After tracing the grey lines, write them correctly in the boxes.

	개	개	개		
	새	새	새		
	게	게	게		
	뇌	뇌	뇌		
	귀	귀	귀		
	쥐	쥐	쥐		

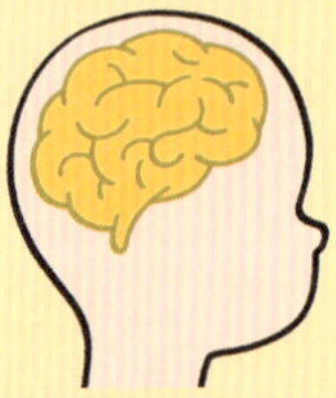

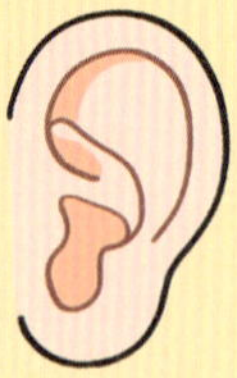

92 * 개 [gae] dog * 새 [sae] bird * 게 [ge] crab * 뇌 [noe] brain * 귀 [gwi] ear * 쥐 [jwi] mouse; rat

Exercise 6

→ These are two-syllable words.
After tracing the grey lines, write them correctly in the boxes.

대	화	대	화		
베	개	베	개		
뷔	페	뷔	페		
시	계	시	계		
돼	지	돼	지		
외	투	외	투		
샤	워	샤	워		

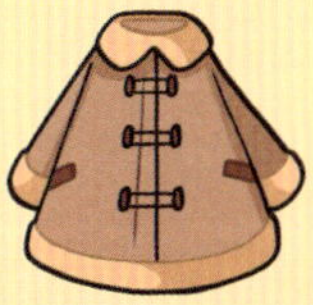

* 대화 [dae-hwa] dialogue * 베개 [be-gae] pillow * 뷔페 [bwi-pe] buffet
* 시계 [si-gye] clock * 돼지 [dwae-ji] pig * 외투 [oe-tu] coat * 샤워 [sya-wo] taking a shower

Exercise 7

→ These are three-syllable and four-syllable words.
After tracing the grey lines, write them correctly in the boxes.

| 재 | 채 | 기 | 재 | 채 | 기 |

| 스 | 웨 | 터 | 스 | 웨 | 터 |

| 꾀 | 꼬 | 리 | 꾀 | 꼬 | 리 |

| 해 | 바 | 라 | 기 | 해 | 바 | 라 | 기 |

| 스 | 파 | 게 | 티 | 스 | 파 | 게 | 티 |

* 재채기 [jae-chae-gi] sneeze * 스웨터 [seu-we-teo] sweater * 꾀꼬리 [ggoe-ggo-ri] nightingale
* 해바라기 [hae-ba-ra-gi] sunflower * 스파게티 [seu-pa-ge-ti] spagetti

Exercise 8

→ Look at the pictures and write the correct syllables in the boxes.

* 과학자 [gwa-hak-jja] scientist * 과일 [gwa-il] fruit * 계란 [gye-ran] (chicken's) egg
* 계산기 [gye-san-gi] calculator * 세탁기 [se-tak-ggi] washing machine * 세수 [se-su] washing one's face
* 참외 [cha-moe] Oriental melon * 외국인 [oe-gu-gin] foreigner * 바위 [ba-wi] rock * 주사위 [ju-sa-wi] dice
* 주근깨 [ju-geun-ggae] freckle * 깨소금 [ggae-so-geum] ground sesame mixed with salt

Writing the syllables

	ㅐ	ㅒ	ㅔ	ㅖ	ㅘ
ㄱ					
ㄴ					
ㄷ					
ㄹ					
ㅁ					
ㅂ					
ㅅ					

	ㅐ	ㅚ	ㅕ	ㅖ	ㅟ	ㅢ
ㄱ						
ㄴ						
ㄷ						
ㄹ						
ㅁ						
ㅂ						
ㅅ						

Writing the syllables

	ㅐ	ㅒ	ㅔ	ㅖ	ㅘ
ㅇ					
ㅈ					
ㅊ					
ㅋ					
ㅌ					
ㅍ					
ㅎ					

	ㅒ	ㅚ	ㅕ	ㅖ	ㅟ	ㅢ
ㅇ						
ㅈ						
ㅊ						
ㅋ						
ㅌ						
ㅍ						
ㅎ						

Writing the syllables

	ㅐ	ㅔ	ㅘ	ㅙ
ㄲ				
ㄸ				
ㅃ				
ㅆ				
ㅉ				

	ㅚ	ㅕ	ㅖ	ㅟ	ㅢ
ㄲ					
ㄸ					
ㅃ					
ㅆ					
ㅉ					

Writing the words

개	구	리	새	우	채	소

그	네	세	모	케	이	크

과	자	대	화	게	돼	지

괴	물	뇌	참	외	열	쇠

궤	도	사	마	귀	바	퀴

쥐	가	위	바	위	의	사

무	늬	샤	워	주	근	깨

꾀	꼬	리	해	바	라	기

'더 콜링'은 언어 학습과 여행에 관심이 많은 모임입니다.
언어란 소통의 도구와 기회라는 신조로,
그것을 염두에 두고 책을 만들고 있습니다.
언어 익히기에 유난히 흥미를 보이는 아이를 키우며
언제, 어떻게 한글 쓰기를 가르칠까 고민하던 때가 있었습니다.
쓸 수 있기 전, 3~4세에는 글자를 이미지화하여 익히도록
했지만, 어느 순간 아이 스스로 자모음의 결합 원리를 깨달아
글자를 습득하게 되었습니다.
아이의 한글 교육을 위해 고민하는 많은 부모들을 보며,
< 하루하루 한글쓰기 > 시리즈를 기획하였고, 외국인에게
한글을 가르친 경험과 다른 사람들에게 도움이 되기 바라는
노하우를 담았습니다.

The Calling is a group keen on learning foreign languages and traveling.
We believe that language is a tool of communication and opportunity, and we make books with that in mind. I was thinking about my life a few years back, when and how I had taught Hangeul to my daughter who was particularly interested in learning languages. At the age of 2 to 3 years old, before she could write, she was able to learn letters by imagining them. Then almost suddenly, she could make the letters by herself because she understood how to combine the characters, the consonants and vowels.
I often encounter parents who are worried about their children's Hangeul learning and so I made this series <Day-by-Day Writing Korean Hangeul>. It includes my own experience with teaching Hangeul to foreigners, know-how I hope will benefit others.

하루하루 한글쓰기 ❹ English ver.

Day-by-Day Writing Korean Hangeul ❹
One-syllable blocks without a final consonant Ⅲ

1st Edition published	2021.8.20.
1st Edition printed	2021.8.10.
written by	The Calling
supervised by	Colin Moore
edited by	Eunkyung Kim
copy-edited by	Jeeyoung Lee
designed by	IndigoBlue
illustrated by	Jeongim Seo
voice actor	Hyunjung Um
voice recording by	BRIDGE CODE
publisher	Kyung-a Cho
published by	LanguageBooks (101-90-85278, 2008.7.10.)
address	208 Bellavista, (390-14, Hapjeong-dong) 31, Poeun-ro 2na-gil, Mapo-gu, Seoul, Korea
telephone	+82-2-406-0047
fax	+82-2-406-0042
e-mail	languagebooks@hanmail.net
mp3 free download	blog.naver.com/languagebook
ISBN	979-11-5635-169-6 (73710)
Price	KRW11,000

©LanguageBooks, 2021

All rights reserved.
No part of this publication may be reproduced or transmitted in any form or by any means without written permission of the publisher.
For information regarding permission, write to Language Books.
The wrong book will be changed at the place of purchase.